My Seven Other Mothers

My Seven Other Mothers

A Journey of Transformation

Lenetta Raysha Lee

Copyright © 2011 by Lenetta Raysha Lee.

Library of Congress Control Number: 2011902832
ISBN: Hardcover   978-1-4568-7389-9
                 Softcover   978-1-4568-7388-2
                 Ebook   978-1-4568-7390-5

This book was printed in the United States of America.

To order additional copies of this book, contact:
Xlibris Corporation
1-888-795-4274
www.Xlibris.com
Orders@Xlibris.com
89773

CONTENTS

"Let me wear the day
Well so when it reaches you
You will enjoy it."

Sonia Sanchez

Egyptian Lotus

Identity. Consciousness.
Reawakening of the mind.
Africanity.
Who am I?
Self-Knowledge.
Truth.
I am me!

Mindfulness. Grace.
Kindness.
Forgiveness.
Practice.
Connected.
Embracing the pain.
Learning to be still.
I am one with God!

Socialization. Process.
Inner Freedom.
Inner Peace.
Rituals. Traditions. Customs.
Believing.
Spiritual Development.
Holistic.
Enlightenment.
I am awake; I am free!

Egyptian Lotus

FOREWORD

One knee does not bring up a child.
—African proverb

Mothering is a central and vital aspect of our lives. Simultaneously, it's a sensitive and complex issue for many people to discuss. The story, *My Seven Mothers*, however, challenges us to revisit our understanding of mothers. As we enter into the lives of these women/mothers, we undoubtedly will notice their unique inner and influential powers.

Unfortunately, in the Western culture, we tend to limit our experience of mothering solely onto the biological mother. In *My Seven Mothers*, the reader will enjoy the rhythm and cosmic beauty of an expansive and more communal concept of motherhood. Each of these seven mothers reminds us to become more mindful of the relationships that we encounter on a daily basis. Because within these relationships, we just might find the resources we need to fulfill our purpose in life.

Truly an intimate narrative, *My Seven Mothers* is storytelling with a purpose. Its primary intention is to provide others with the insight and wisdom to begin healing. As well, the fundamental question this book poses is not so much who is a mother, but rather what is the function of a mother.

So be still, open your mind, and enjoy the journey. More importantly, look inward and embrace the fruits of my seven mothers.

Aseyoga.com

INTRODUCTION

"The best thing you can do is to be a woman and stand before the world and speak your heart."

A spiritual renaissance resonates within me. This feeling ignites the energy and inspiration for me to write these words.

Creating this story is twofold; on one level I want to emphasize the profound effect seven American women had on my embodiment eventually enlightenment. I call these seven women my "seven other mothers."

Embodiment is that sense of the spirit moving, traveling, through the body—whereas enlightenment is releasing the energy of the body. Awakening the body must occur before development can be achieved. My seven other mothers possessed an intense level of caring for me. Through this intense level of unconditional caring, each mother served to awaken my senses and enrich my life.

On another level, I want to share my experiences to make visible a path toward enlightenment. Life is suffering. The life goal is to look inward, observe oneself and accept what life brings with an open mind and spirit. My other mothers guided me along a path that showed me a way out of suffering—into peace. I traveled a path, birth to adulthood, of awakening.

My other mothers added value to my life; I surrendered to their personal messages, allowing the spirit to flow through me freely. The journey traveled with my other mothers was a spiritual practice.

This memoir illuminates each mother and the relationship we experienced overtime. Each divine mother, guru, talked to me about me; each actively listened to what I had to say. The lessons created a vessel or pathway toward freedom, a way of becoming alive and free. Each divine mother possessed a rhythm and a spirit, which sings inside me today. Because of my other mothers, I am able to love and be loved, trust and be trusted.

Essentially, my seven other mothers are the source and foundation of my life. As expressed in Maat, each taught me explicitly seven virtues: truth, balance, reciprocity, justice, order, morality, harmony, and propriety.

My seven other mothers prepared a foundation for me to live a joyful life. Everyone must identify his or her other mothers and sanction the process of transformation.

For this memoir, I focus on seven beautiful women. I begin and end this journey of transformation with my parents, Albie Lucile Lee, my mother, and Luvinia Olive Burruss, my grandmother, followed by Ella Forbes, Sheila Sawyer, Gladys Renwick, Pearl Jean Kennedy Mullett, and Denise Walden.

ALBIE

"The soul is a tiny thing that brings us peace and joy when we let it swim."

Albie Lucile Lee is my first role model and teacher; I am my mother's seventh child. My mother shaped my heart, identity, and culture through right and wrong teachings. She gave me the opportunity to develop mindfulness and the right to examine deeper.

My mother is an independent, medium-boned, brown-skinned lady, who is rarely seen without a stylish hat. She is soft spoken, and she has incredible insight. My mother loves to laugh, and she uses words creatively to be funny. Managing cryptograms, with one vowel, while raising seven children was one of her favorite pastimes.

At an early age, on any given night, I would sometimes observe my mother reading or writing. In fact, it was not uncommon to see my mother reading two books at one time in the well-lit kitchen, bedroom, or living room. I remember watching the bookmarks in the books move closer and closer to the end of each book. My mother was an avid reader, writer, and lover of music. The house felt, smelled, and tasted of the various genres of music throughout the day.

My mother wrote to change the community. She wrote several editorials on issues relevant to the neighborhood. My mother used writing to influence and affect her surroundings. She also served on several community organizations including the local Democratic Party.

Despite her long days, nightly my mother always prepared dinner between five and six o'clock, and we were always ready. My mother was innovative in the kitchen. One night of the week we might have mashed potatoes, and later in the week the leftover mashed potatoes became potato fritters. Leftover corn was often mixed in pancake batter. Some clothes were handmade, but most passed down from one sister to the next. My mother did not waste food or money.

For the most part, my mother was quiet at home, but when she spoke, we listened. I observed my mother work through everyday life; I desired to be just like her.

My mother allowed my siblings and me to participate in the various activities that Lincoln University offered their student body including cultural events and convocations.

Throughout my childhood, I met prominent African American persons like Sonia Sanchez, Maya Angelou, Nikki Giovanni, Jesse Jackson, and Cicely Tyson. My sister Judith and I, in a buddy system, attended yoga, fencing, martial arts, and chess classes on Lincoln University's campus. The martial arts instructor, Wanda Robinson from Wilmington, Delaware, whom we see at least once year, taught by the acclaimed martial arts instructor Jock, still influences us. We studied chess under Professor Horowitz who later during my sophomore year was my professor of philosophy. My mother used Lincoln University as a vehicle to expand the identity and culture of her children.

One day, I decided to smoke a cigarette. I found a cigarette butt in an ashtray, and I searched for a box of matches. Glancing back and forth, like an owl, I walked out the front door and ran toward the backyard. In the backyard, I squatted down, not to be seen, and I lit the cigarette and began smoking. Just when I concluded I was real cool, my mother drove by the house. I could have died. She stared down my throat as she drove past. I released the matches and cigarette and ran as fast as I could back into the house. I began to pace. "Maybe she did not see me." I prayed.

My mother came into the house and continued with her routine. She behaved normally, and so did I. My mother behaved so normally, I was convinced she did not see me smoking the cigarette butt. Later that night, without warning, my mother called me to the back of the house. She asked me why I was smoking a cigarette. I offered no explanation. This is the only time I can remember getting a beating from my mother, and I have never picked up another cigarette.

After graduating magna cum laude from Lincoln University in Pennsylvania, I chose to matriculate at the Ohio State University graduate school of education. I earned a full scholarship with stipend. I arrived in Columbus, Ohio, mid-August 1985. I called my mother several times daily. In fact, I cried every day begging to return home. I passionately explained to my mother in detail to make my point. All of Lincoln University could fit into the Ohio State football stadium, and Ohio State could still host a sold-out game. This was not the gently flowing pond of Lincoln University; this was an ocean, and I was afraid.

I equated size with quality. My mother took her time with me. She kept me occupied by asking well-thought-out questions. "Have you met any of your new classmates?" "How does the house look?" The questions were comforting; however, I continued to cry and complain. I insisted I should return home, teach in a local school, and complete a graduate degree closer to home. During every call home, my mother continued to inquire about my surroundings, and in between the phone calls, my mother wrote me letters. Finally, my mother suggested, "Lenetta, make yourself familiar with your new school, walk to each class, and call me later tonight." I did as I was told, and two days later I was prepared for my classes. The rest is history. I returned home a year later with a master's degree in reading and language arts and a reading specialist certification.

The most influential and learned lesson my mother taught me was when I initially returned home from graduate school. After hanging out with old friends, most of the night, I wandered into my mother's house. Without interruption, my mother said, "Lenetta, you are on a different level. You cannot hang out with old friends all night." As she walked around me never skipping a beat, I appeared as though I was listening; my first thoughts were I could not wait to move out. I honestly thought my mother was merely attempting to make me think, act, and essentially be better than my friends. Of course, in the end, she was right.

Off to graduate school again, this time to pursue a doctorate of philosophy, I asked my mother what she thought about my pursuing a degree in African and African American studies. There was much discussion pertaining to the degree I should seek because I already had two degrees in education. It appeared the obvious and easiest approach would be to obtain a doctorate in education. The quandary was I already completed a master's degree in reading, 51 credits. Moreover, I taught undergraduate- and graduate-level reading courses at three universities: Lincoln University, St. Joseph's University, and Eastern Mennonite University all in Pennsylvania.

Thus, I decided to pursue a degree in the first African and African American studies program. I needed to be challenged. I desired to combine my research interest, African American children's literature and black studies.

My mother informed me she knew I would do well with a PhD in any area. That was not her concern. She said, "If you pursue a degree in African American studies, remember I named you Lenetta Raysha Lee, and I would appreciate it if you did not change your name."

I defended my dissertation in the spring of 2000. Obviously, I did not change my name. My mother named me for my cousin Lena and my grandfather Albert Ray Taylor. I am immensely proud of my name. Hearing or calling my name provides me strength.

Naming a child is a spiritual process. Hearing people call one's name, and by one calling one's own name, one ascends into one's destiny. The ancient African naming practice is the beginning of a unique initiation to a young person's life. Initially, the child is told his name. The child is then presented by name along with path to the villagers. Thus, the child's destiny or course is revealed. The child is now, with both name and destiny, ready to live. It is the responsibility of the villagers to monitor and facilitate the child along the path for a lifetime. If the child strays away from the path, it is the villagers' commitment to place the child back on the original path. If the child fails, the village fails. This act exemplifies the ancient African proverb "It takes a village to raise a child."

My birth mother gave me the gift of life, and residing near her today is an ongoing and continuous spiritual journey. Her lessons about right and wrong throughout my life were consistent and based on truth.

I thank my mother for embracing my other mothers and, more specifically, pointing out and presenting to me successful women. Essentially, my mother grounded me deep into the earth, rooted, and she watched me grow from the earth like an Egyptian lotus flower. Effectively, she taught me how to fly but not until she was sure I was prepared for the long journey of life.

From my mother's womb and into adulthood, my other mothers continued to nourish me spiritually. Today as I work on me, I practice daily to ensure continued unfolding.

ELLA

"When you really pay attention, everything is your teacher."

I met Ella while a senior at the Oxford Area High School in Oxford, Pennsylvania. The assigned classroom teacher introduced Ella as the student teacher. It was vocabulary class, and I was currently failing. I was not motivated; I had a genuine dislike for the assigned classroom teacher. The classroom teacher liked to embarrass students, and it frightened me. In fact, it deepened my shyness and essentially caused me to be an introvert.

At first sight, I did not trust Ella. She looked too old to be a student teacher. When she began to teach, I placed myself in the back of the classroom behind a larger classmate. Essentially, I hid. Initially, I gave Ella an extremely difficult time questioning and challenging her every move. Each day she taught, her gestures, body, and eyes would search for me.

Soon, it was Ella I rose for each morning with a smile on my face prepared for school. I could not wait for vocabulary class. Despite the fact that I continued to give Ella a hard time, not listening and being disruptive in class, Ella and I began to engage in small talk.

Ella continued to reach out to me. I smiled inwardly, inner peace, as I reflected on her efforts. Eventually, Ella worked through my false hatred, and we became friends. Because of Ella, I was able to pass vocabulary class and graduate.

As time passed, Ella gave me so much more. Ella's impact on my life is tremendous. She has been a quiet influence in my life from the moment we meet. We did not engage in conversations in terms of right and wrong; the conversations pertained to mindfulness. I remember several conversations with Ella about my future. Relentlessly she investigated what I wanted to do with my life. She told me she wanted to be a librarian; I told her she was too pretty. When Ella completed her student teaching practicum, to my surprise, she began working at the Langston Hughes Memorial Library on the campus of Lincoln University.

Ella wore her hair in a bun with small-wired framed reading glasses. Her dark almond skin tone fits her warm face. Her voice is soft; her words are strong. One of her favorite pastimes is working in her garden.

I arrived on Lincoln University's campus in 1981 to find Ella working in the library. I sat in her office daily talking; she listened. Not once did she say she did not have time for me.

She was an active listener, and I can remember feeling at ease every time I left her job. I told Ella story after story of my childhood. She listened unconditionally; however, once my story was spoken, there was no repeating the story ever. There was no need to repeat the story. It was over. Ella never turned me away despite showing up at her residence or place of employment daily.

Ella's house was full of books and love; I visited her home for hours. Her home was a sanctuary full of many flowers, many plants, and many trees. There were water gardens and ponds placed strategically throughout the lawn.

One single small pond was one of my son, Langston's, fishing holes. I paraded my nephews and my son to Ella's house and job; I wanted them to be in her space, hear her words, and meet her energy.

Ella taught me negative thoughts affected one's life, so I practiced thinking and speaking positive thoughts while I was with her. This practice became an obsession. This obsession led to forgiveness; forgiveness is living.

Ella built on my concept of self by being herself. Through Ella, I was able to see more, feel more, hear more, and know more. Ella taught me mindfulness by being mindful. When my heart and tongue did not match, she would comment with her eyes only, "Watch what you say." It was through Ella's teachings that I learned forgiveness. She did not let me speak or even consider certain things. She wiped negative pictures from my heart and mind by listening. Ella knew I was learning; she could see the changes in me.

Years later, Dr. Forbes talked me into pursuing a PhD from the first African and African American Studies Department at Temple University in Philadelphia, Pennsylvania. Accepted, Dr. Forbes became my advisor. Ella whispered in my ear during the new student orientation, "Welcome to a journey of a lifetime." As I walked out of the auditorium feeling proud, there stood at the top of the room the poet Sonia Sanchez. The feeling was overwhelming; I knew I was embarking on a brand-new experience.

In 2000, Dr. Forbes lost her son, Erin Dudley Forbes. My son was four, and prior to giving birth I talked about opening my own school. Once I gave birth I decided, establishing a school would be too much while raising a young African American male child. When Erin was shot and killed, in his honor and to honor his parents, I asked if I could name the school for Erin.

Erin's parents granted me permission. Work to establish the first charter school in southeastern Pennsylvania, the Erin Dudley Forbes Charter School, was initiated. Erin Dudley Forbes Charter School, located in Oxford, Pennsylvania, educated many students, parents, and community for nine years.

Ella's historical consciousness and mindfulness filtered from her into me. Upon this foundation of consciousness, I am able to create and be creative.

SHEILA

"There is purpose behind you."

I waited patiently for Sheila to visit my grandmother during the week and on the weekends. I watched as they played pinochle until the early morning light. Sheila never wore the same outfit twice. At a young age, her attitude and style attracted me. I observed her carefully listening to every word like a mother bird watches over her baby birds. She was brilliant, understandable, and accurate.

Sheila is a short, petite woman with short hair dyed reddish blond. Her skin tone is golden brown like the color of coffee with two creams. Her voice is strong and assertive.

I met Sheila over forty years ago. Like my mother, Sheila instilled in me the difference between right and wrong. Sheila reinforced my mother's right and wrong lessons. Her manner was more candid and pointed. "Bones, you cannot do that!" Sheila affectionately called me Bones, a nickname given to me by my grandmother.

I observed Sheila carefully, and I heard every word she spoke. Her conversations were significant; she was intelligent.

Asa Hilliard, educator, talks about the benefits of hearing and listening. Hilliard posits that a hearer is a ready, receptive focused student.

Perception and listening is the penetration of the deeper meaning of the message. Ultimately, the learner, hearer, and listener perform in three ways: role model, obedient, and devoted. I was all three in Sheila's presence and, therefore, continued to be with all my other mothers.

Sheila moved from the local community. Once I learned how to drive, I traveled late at night to Sheila's house with my friends crammed in the small two-door car. Like Ella, she never turned me away. Typically, after a late event in the university, fraternity or sorority dance or step show, I would venture off to Sheila's. Her late-night lessons penetrated my mind. My immaturity would not let me convey to Sheila how much her messages helped me, so instead, I never agreed with her. In fact, I always told her she was wrong. This did not stop her from speaking, conveying the message repeatedly.

Sheila, writer and educator, possessed the secret to education's potential. She insisted over and over again I move away from Lincoln University to become educated. As I pursued my graduate studies, Sheila embraced me. In graduate school, she encouraged me with regular phone calls and letters. Sheila stretched me academically and socially.

Recently, I asked Sheila if she had the letters we shared while I was in graduate school. She paused and finally said with a smile, "Love letters." I asked her what she meant, and she said my letters read like love letters. Instantly, I understood what she meant. She filled my heart and soul with unconditional love; my letters exuded the same feeling.

Sheila is a vital source of light in my life. Currently, she is editing my dissertation for publication, and most recently she spoke to the Frederick Douglass Institute scholars at Cheyney University, where

I currently teach in the Humanities and Communication Arts Department. Her lecture expressed the importance of Frederick Douglass' life, careers in English, and multicultural education.

Sheila, like Ella, has an extensive home library. I visited Sheila's library often while writing my dissertation. Sheila provided me a relaxed, peaceful place to learn and sleep. With writer's block paralyzing my thoughts, I would quickly pack up my writing tools and drive to Sheila's house to write and essentially rest. Again, she was always available.

My son, Langston, refers to Sheila as Aunt Sheila, and he smiles wide and often when she tells him Langston Hughes is her favorite author.

Sheila represents the fulfillment of one's potential. Whenever I would visit her, she would give me a gift. We did not know at the time, but she was giving me the gift of life.

Sheila constantly reminded me of what I was doing right and what I was doing wrong, a balancing act. Too often she reminded me of Jiminy Cricket from the fairy tale Pinocchio exercising her right to sit on my shoulder and guide my life. Sheila taught me enormous possibilities by expressing her own unlimited potential. In my mind, there was nothing Sheila could not execute.

Case in point, I was not surprised when Sheila delivered an extremely powerful message. I was a sophomore at Lincoln University; it was my job to secure the speaker for the annual weeklong Alpha Kappa Alpha Sorority Incorporated events. I procrastinated, so I contacted Sheila because I knew she would say yes.

She agreed to be the guest speaker for the event despite the truth that I did not give her much time to prepare. Sheila called several times asking me to explain what I wanted the message to say. We continued to play phone tag.

I can remember feeling annoyed at the numerous phone calls with the same question: "What should I say?" I emphasized to Sheila that the message should be around understanding and healing. The morning of the event, I sat in the front pew of the Mary Dod Brown Chapel located on Lincoln University's campus anticipating Sheila's message.

While waiting for Sheila to speak, I fell asleep. I was extremely tired from the weeklong activities and the party the night before. I was sleeping well when I awoke with a joggle. I shook my head from side to side like a bird after drinking from a birdbath. I immediately knew Sheila's message was for me, and the message was from a mutual friend. As Sheila continued, tears streamed down my face. Early fall of the same year, a mutual friend, Joan Mayo, died of lupus. I watched Joan grow weaker and weaker; ultimately, Joan was unable to return to work. I called Joan at least once a week to stay in touch. The last conversation I had with Joan she insisted I visit; she said she had something worthwhile to tell me. I told her I would stop by on Saturday. I did not go. Joan passed Tuesday.

I called for God, and I pleaded to give Joan a way to deliver the message. I also prayed for forgiveness for missing the message. Smiling each night before bed, after praying during the day for the message, and then saying to myself softly but seriously, "Joan, do not tell me at night."

Joan chose Sheila to deliver that message. When I first heard the message some twenty-seven years ago, I thought, *Okay, Joan wants me to accept God unconditionally, accept God, and to refrain from practicing "crisis Christianity."* The message was clear, to seek and trust God. Today, the message is even more significant. Twenty-seven years later, the message has become much deeper. Joan revealed the divine potential in me and the need to demonstrate godlike ways. She wanted me to know that God resides in me.

She wanted me to realize my inner potential and walk a path of righteousness. By demonstrating acts of kindness and compassion, God becomes a living reality.

As a reminder, I keep a copy of scripture in my box of letters, and from time to time I reminisce on the many lessons. Joan Mayo is an example of the "other mother" who appears for a moment. I am grateful.

GLADYS

"I am who I am because of who we all are."

Mrs. Renwick resided in the small, vibrant, affluent African American community of Lincoln University in Pennsylvania with her husband, each employed by Lincoln University. Mrs. Renwick was the chief dietitian, and Mr. Renwick was the school's barber. Mr. and Mrs. Renwick did not have any children of their own, but their home was always full of young and older people, an intergenerational meeting place.

I started working for Mrs. Renwick when I was ten, pulling weeds in her beautiful vast garden that surrounded her home. By age twelve, I was trained to clean the three-story house. It gave me immense pleasure, despite the sun, rain, sleet, or snow, to awaken early Saturday mornings, until the age twenty-one, to work for Mrs. Renwick.

When I was young, I traveled by bike to Mrs. Renwick's house, and when I did not have a bike I walked. Later, when I learned how to drive, I drove. In autumn, I rode on my bike through the many beautiful leaves, and in the winter I slid through the snow. In the fall, I skipped, through the leaves, gathering and jumping, to make the journey peaceful. In the winter, I stopped to make snow angels.

There was nothing more exciting than to ride my bike through the leaves and slam on the brakes and slide and slide into another world. The weekly trip to Mrs. Renwick's house was always a perfect journey.

Mrs. Renwick had a perfectly round bright light-skinned face; She was a heavyset woman with deep dimples set on each side of her tan-colored checks. When I first met her, her hair was mostly gray, and when she transitioned, it was pure white. Mrs. Renwick wore her hair pulled back in a beautiful tightly woven bun. The only time I saw Mrs. Renwick's hair down was when I washed her hair.

Mrs. Renwick kept a long cigarette protruding from the left side of her mouth. The smoke rose leisurely tinting the left corner of her hair blonde. The cigarette and ashes dangled while she spoke. The gray smoke formed a perfect circle horizontally at the tip of the cigarette, and finally the ashes would fall on Mrs. Renwick's shirt or floor.

My first job description was to remove weeds in the flowerbeds. The flowerbeds were beautiful as they wound around the house like a vine or beautiful veranda.

Mrs. Renwick trained me well. She showed me the difference between a weed and a flower, and she gave me a strange tool to remove the weeds out of the earth. She taught me the best clothing to wear to pull weeds comfortably.

Explicit directions and guidance were given until I could be trusted, trusted not to ruin her garden. I was then elevated to cleaning the house. When I was elevated to cleaning the house, a younger child was hired to pull the weeds in the garden, and I could hear Mrs.

Renwick repeating the same directions to the young child that she used with me. Thus, the circle was complete.

While cleaning, I received valuable lessons pertaining to life that I still adhere to today. I can still hear Mrs. Renwick say, "Never use water on the wooden floors, and vacuum slowly to see all the dirt."

Lincoln University was a private all-male institution when Mrs. Renwick was the head dietitian. Mrs. Renwick, although known for her cooking, managing the refractory with an iron fist, and training men, also helped me. While cleaning or visiting Mrs. Renwick, I listened intently to her instructions to the male students and professors who visited her. The rabble continued at Mrs. Renwick's house over scotch and soul food.

Mrs. Renwick's house was a beautiful three-story home with hardwood floors and oriental carpets and a large backyard. There were three bedrooms upstairs, with the master bedroom on the first floor.

There were three bathrooms. The basement is where Mrs. Renwick spent time painting. Mrs. Renwick's original paintings and African artifacts were all throughout the house. Mrs. Renwick was a thriving creative artist. She usually painted flowers and garden scenes. She also enjoyed abstract art as well as framing.

She painted one picture of her husband in his hunting clothes with his rifle over his shoulder. Mrs. Renwick was immensely proud of the portrayal of her husband. I can still see the full, colorful, realistic picture resting on the old wooden easel in the basement. I have one of Mrs. Renwick's paintings on my kitchen wall. The picture is of three bright yellow marigolds. She gifted me the picture when I was in undergraduate school.

I began working for Mrs. Renwick earning ten dollars a week for pulling weeds. Later, I earned twenty dollars a week cleaning the house along with a present of fifty dollars every Christmas. With the twenty dollars, I would buy essentials so my mother did not have to, or I would give my classmates greasy French fries from the snack bar. The greasy fries filled stomachs and souls for four years. We were all thankful.

Trained to set up the mighty artificial green Christmas tree in the large living room adjacent the bay window, Mrs. Renwick developed a method for putting up the tree. She insisted I follow the procedure as she prescribed.

Until I was thirty, I put the Christmas tree up the day after Thanksgiving. I placed each bulb on the tree strategically. The Christmas bulbs from Mrs. Renwick's youth were different sizes and colors. There was one bulb that was Mr. Renwick's favorite, and when he died, the ornament became Mrs. Renwick's favorite.

The ornament was a small open baby blue plastic gazebo. There was a metal abstract element inside. I placed the bulb on the front of the tree, for visibility, and underneath a light, so the metal object could change. When it was time to place the bulb on the tree, I called Mrs. Renwick into the room, and I would announce, "It is time to place Mr. Renwick's favorite bulb on the tree." Mrs. Renwick would venture into the living room, sit down, beam, and behold the annual event. Typically, around mid-January, I returned to Mrs. Renwick's house to dismantle the tree. I started by removing the various strands of lights, followed by each bulb. I carefully wrapped each bulb in tissue paper and placed it back into its original box.

While Mrs. Renwick's house remained the same, Mrs. Renwick was getting older, and I was maturing. Despite my commitment to my schoolwork, I continued to clean on Saturday mornings. The opportunity to dance all night on Friday evenings was also fascinating. I loved to dance—a relationship that has continued throughout my life. Soon I began to plan my weekend activities around my responsibility to Mrs. Renwick. She did not approve of me cleaning on Sunday. For the most part, I cleaned on my scheduled time.

When Mrs. Renwick was no longer able to manage her home on her own, she moved to an apartment in the nearby town. I continued to clean and pull weeds as well as set up her Christmas tree. When she was unable to manage by herself alone, she lived in the local nursing home. I visited her daily or as often as I could.

Mrs. Renwick later died in that local nursing home. She gifted me her platinum wedding band. I wear it on my right thumb. Through Mrs. Renwick, I learned some lifelong lessons.

Mrs. Renwick did not teach me how to cook despite her enthusiasm and ability. I can only guess she did not want me to focus on cooking. Perhaps she thought I should do something else.

Mrs. Renwick taught me the difference between a weed and a flower. This comparison became a measuring stick for many similar comparisons. Today my house and yard are full of the various types of beautiful flowers, and I love fresh flowers in my home. The process of learning how to remove weeds and clean Mrs. Renwick's house was an invaluable lesson for a young woman to understand. I mastered and crafted the process—a lifelong strategy.

There was always this interconnectedness with everyone who visited Mrs. Renwick. She represented Ubuntu, ancestral like,—meaning a person who is open and available for others, and always affirming others. Ubuntu defines the individual, in this case Mrs. Renwick, and her relationships with others. Ubuntu teaches that a person, essentially, is a person through others, one who develops by behaving with compassion, one who behaves with humanity. By opening the ways for others, Mrs. Renwick lived a full, good, and meaningful life.

PEARL JEAN

"Graceful."

At Lincoln University, where I studied early childhood education, one of my favorite pastimes was sitting on the little white brick wall outside University Hall and wait for Dr. Pearl Jean Kennedy Mullett to walk to work. She and her husband resided directly across the street from the university in a university home.

Watching Dr. Mullett brought me inner peace and happiness. I was enamored with her stillness, gracefulness, all I could think is "Wow, what a lady." We did not speak at all. Most days we only shared a glance and a smile. Unknown to Dr. Kennedy, I waited and watched her daily sometimes twice a day. I enjoyed being in her presence even for just a moment. Attracted to her warm gentleness, I sat in the moment, observing.

Dr. Kennedy always wore a small colorful fitted hat. She was a little light brown-skinned woman, and she spoke with a southern drawl.

It was cleaning Mrs. Renwick's house that afforded me a closer relationship with Dr. Kennedy. When Dr. Kennedy left her husband, she moved into Mrs. Renwick's house during the week, and on the weekends she went to her seaside home in New Jersey.

Dr. Kennedy slept in the smallest of the three bedrooms upstairs. Mrs. Renwick informed me not to go into her room; however, despite her warnings, I went into her perfume-filled room to dust and reorganize her shoes. Once I realized Dr. Kennedy moved in with Mrs. Renwick, I began to spend more time at Mrs. Renwick's house. Dr. Kennedy and I began to have small conversations about family and school.

I showed no emotion when I began to notice Dr. Kennedy did not return to Mrs. Renwick's. After several weeks, when I was sure Dr. Kennedy did not return to Mrs. Renwick's, I finally ask Mrs. Renwick where she was. Mrs. Renwick told me Dr. Kennedy took a postdoctorate at Harvard University in Boston, Massachusetts. I was speechless, like snow falling in the middle of the night. *Why?* I thought. I suddenly felt confused. Meanwhile, Dr. Kennedy began to send cards to Mrs. Renwick. I began to run to the mailbox at the end of the driveway to get the mail. I used the return address on one of the envelopes, and I began to write. Too my surprise, she wrote me back. We shared several letters while she was in Boston. One letter changed my life.

Recently, while curling my mother's hair and reflecting on my life and memoir, I inquired, "Mom, do you have any of the letters I wrote while in graduate school?" She replied no, she had thrown them all away except the one note where I insisted I was not perfect. We both chuckled. We knew the meaning of that letter. I smiled and continued to curl her hair. Still reflecting, I asked, "Mom, do you remember the letter Dr. Mullett wrote me?"

"Of course, it was the most beautiful letter." My mother inquired, "Do you still have that letter?"

"Yes," I said, reflecting quietly to myself, "that letter changed my life."

In the letter, Dr. Kennedy instructed me to read the book *The Cinderella Complex*. There was urgency in the message. Dr. Kennedy told me I should read the book before I got any older. She explained she wished someone told her about the book before she was her age.

I can remember running across campus, as fast as I could, to the Langston Hughes Memorial Library on Lincoln University's campus to find the book. I ran top speed without stopping. After an extensive search, the Lincoln library did not have the book. I had to use the interlibrary loan system to obtain the book. The book arrived several days later. I read the book in its entirety in one sitting, and I continued to reread the book to ensure I was getting the message.

The Cinderella Complex by Colette Dowling, published in 1981, the same year I entered college, was passed down to me by one of my other mothers. I read *The Cinderella Complex* in its entirety my sophomore year; I was nineteen years old. At the age of forty-seven, I reread the book.

According to Dowling, the Cinderella complex is the strong desire for women to be saved. Dowling contends that women only have one shot at liberation. Dowling continues, "Personal psychological dependency—the deep wish to be taken care of by others—is the chief force holding women down today. I call this the Cinderella Complex—a network of largely repressed attitudes and fears that keeps women in a kind of half-light, retreating from the full use of their minds and creativity. Like Cinderella, women today are still waiting for something external to transform their lives."

Dr. Kennedy found herself caught up in a Cinderella complex web of confusion after separating from her husband. The fantastic news is she passed the message to the younger generation. Reading *The Cinderella Complex* the first time revealed an emotion I felt before. Reading the book elevated my attitude toward being in a relationship while studying. I came to the realization that I could only be a friend with any of my male counterparts.

I remained a virgin until I was twenty-one years of age. Free from the sensation and expectation of having a boyfriend while in, undergraduate or graduate, school, I excelled. Essentially, after reading *The Cinderella Complex*, the cliche of meeting a man while in school did not ring true for me.

The last time I was in Dr. Mullett's presence was at the Lincoln University graduate center in Philadelphia, Pennsylvania. The graduate students surprised me with a baby shower. I was with child, thirty-six years of age, teaching graduate education courses and preparing to defend my dissertation. Dr. Kennedy sat quietly in the multipurpose room as food and gifts were plentiful. I watched her like I watched her so many times before sitting outside Lincoln Hall. Once again we only shared a glance and a smile. I knew she approved. When I turned back around, she was gone.

DENISE

"Let us guide our destiny."

She wore a beautiful silver ankh, symbolizing life, around her neck and some silver bracelets on her right arm. The silver bracelets on her arm sang when she walked or moved. Denise Walden was from Pittsburgh, Pennsylvania, and a Lincoln University graduate, class of 1975. Walden was a psychology major. It is Walden who stretched my heart. When I reflect on my relationship with Walden, I think transparency, peace, and growth.

Walden was a heavyset light-skinned woman with a tight brown curly Afro. Because her skin was pale, she wore a little makeup. She possessed a kind and gentle smile. Walden was always smiling, and her laugh was infectious. Walden's energy was affectionate. Like with Ella, I presented my nephews and son to Walden as much as possible. Her presence was authentic, and her speech conscious. Walden like Ella understood the power of words, language, and text.

Walden touched my heart from high school until her transition in 2003. Prior to joining the Lincoln University Upward Bound family in 1982, I attended Walden's recruitment sessions at the local high school.

Walden attended the local high schools in the area to recruit students for the Lincoln University Upward Bound Program. I had no intentions on applying for Upward Bound; I only attended the sessions to be in Walden's presence.

A freshman at Lincoln University, I interviewed with Ms. Walden for a tutor counselor position with the Lincoln University Upward Bound Program. Excited and extremely nervous, the first time I interviewed, I was not hired; however, I continued to place myself near Walden.

In fact, I began to volunteer for the program. The first time I interviewed with Walden, she told me I did not get the job because I was too young. She told me later she was waiting to see if I would return to interview the following year. I did, and I got the job. The second interview was easier. While working with the Lincoln University program with Walden as the assistant director, she crafted my work ethic and discipline.

Subsequently, I worked with Lincoln University's Upward Bound Program under Walden's guidance for approximately sixteen years. I worked in various positions from tutor counselor to center supervisor, reading specialist, and educator.

Walden never appeared tired, and she used every minute of the day. She paid attention to what she was doing. Forget multitasking. She gave each task her undivided attention; this is how she treated her employees, teachers, and students. Walden treated pertinent matters, one by one, with reasonableness and calmness. Walden was focused and full of life.

As soon as I got writer's block or frustrated while writing, I would pack up my writing needs and walk to Walden's office. Walden provided me with everything I needed to write most significant, atmosphere.

My creative juices always seemed to restart in her presence, and we worked until she decided it was time to go home. Unlike Ella and Sheila, I never went to Walden's house. She was private, and she made it known. Walden only invited me to her house to pick up newspaper or magazine articles she insisted I take. She would meet me at the door with an armful of magazines and newspapers, shove them in my arms, and shut the door. Walden kept everything.

Walden was the first person I confided in that I was expecting. She was ecstatic. Pregnant with my first child, on sabbatical, an unwed mother, and teacher at the age of thirty-six, was challenging.

I was on sabbatical from my full-time job teaching first grade in the local school district, and I held the part-time position of center supervisor for the Lincoln University Upward Bound Program. Ms. Walden was my immediate supervisor. We discussed at length how and when I should tell the elementary school principal, the Upward Bound students, and their parents, I was expecting. She coached me, relieving my fears.

It was because of Walden that I viewed the film *Sankofa* for the first time. We traveled to Sixty-ninth Street in Upper Darby for the viewing. The movie *Sankofa* changed my life, and it continues to change me as I view it at least once a year with my undergraduate students at Cheyney University.

Always a source of encouragement, it was Walden with whom I shared many late-night conversations, solving all the educational problems of the world.

Walden possessed a beautiful spirit. Initially, when she told me she was going back to Pittsburgh, I did not understand. Walden was serene and spiritual about her move. She said it was time, like the concept Sankofa, for her to return home. While I was terribly disappointed and, in fact, saddened, I knew it was time for Walden to return home. Despite the distance, we continued spending time on the phone talking for hours.

When Walden relocated, I searched for educational conferences in her area. I submitted an abstract to speak at the University of Pittsburgh at the Greensburg Millstein Library's Annual Children's Literature Conference.

I searched for a conference in the Pittsburgh area to present my dissertation topic, history of African American children's literature, and see Walden. Finally, I was invited to speak at the Greensburg Millstein Library Annual Children's Literature. After the conference, Walden and I meet on the Pennsylvania turnpike. Walden's car was full of reading materials and motivational posters she insisted I needed.

We talked outside near the cars for several hours with my car facing the direction I needed to travel. That was the last time I saw Walden face-to-face. We continued to talk by phone until her untimely transition in 2003. In fact, we spoke a few days before she passed.

Walden had evolved considerably. She stopped smoking, and one by one she dismissed the contradictions in her life; she encouraged me to do the same. Walden could not execute right speech and action if her heart is full of contradictions.

She held on to the position of moral and right even when others did not, without judging. Walden had strong convictions; she stood by them. Liberating her of the contradictions continued to let her grow emotionally and socially. Walden was changing in terms of identity, mindfulness, and socialization, and I was too.

Walden compelled me to be me, despite the demands for change.

Walden confirmed my identity, and she made me fully aware of the contradictions in my life. She taught me self-reflection and self-inquiry. In my own mind, I began to question why I did certain things. This process of self-realization assisted me in understanding how my mind worked. This consciousness about consciousness, meta-awareness, taught me right conduct and character.

LUVINIA

"There is no way to happiness, happiness is the way."

Luvinia Olive Burruss, affectionately known as Sissy and Nana Fanny, was a restaurateur in the community of Lincoln University for over forty years. My grandmother owned and operated the first African American restaurant, Ye Ole Lions Inn, in the community. While alive at the age of ninety-five, she did not know that the United States of America had elected its first African American president.

My grandmother was her mother's seventh child, and I my mother's seventh child. We referred to each other as seven and seven. Born for success is what my grandmother stressed to all family members and me. I believed her. Believing is the solution.

Determined, confident, caring, and kind, Nana was a petite woman with cinnamon, flawless skin tone. In her younger days, she wore stylish wigs as well as her natural hair. I cannot remember a time when my grandmother was angry or upset. She seemed to drift in and out of the day, producing much, taking what life brought her. Nana was not a sleeper; it seems she was always awake.

As owner of a restaurant, Nana Fanny fed many bodies and souls including mine. She opened her home all hours of the night. She always had a word of wisdom for the Lincoln University students.

Nana Fanny was a giver. She gave to everyone who needed. In fact, we had to watch because she would give away everything if she could. Nana Fanny found faith in the world. She boldly reached out and confidently embraced the world and shared in it.

As a youngster, I traveled from the city to the country to my grandmother's house for summer vacation. When my parents divorced at the age of six, we moved to Lincoln University.

We installed a four-bedroom mobile home on my grandmother's two acres of land. My grandmother resided next door to me all my young and adult life. My grandmother's back door faced my front door, only minutes apart. We were in and out of her house all the time. I remember one morning I wanted some candy, so I snuck in the restaurant, and I missed the school bus. Boy, was I in trouble.

I vividly remember the only time my grandmother spanked me. We were in the restaurant. Nana JuJu, my grandmother's oldest sister, was visiting, and Nana Fanny thought I was being disrespectful to Nana JuJu.

I was in the back room, and Nana Fanny was behind the front counter; she was dipping ice cream for a customer. She thought I called Nana JuJu by her first name, Julia. Nana Fanny talked to me at length about what I did wrong, and then she spanked me.

My grandmother had an enormous impact on my life. She was a restaurateur and I a teacher. Despite the remarkably different professions, I believe my grandmother, and I shared the same life calling. She delivered relevant messages using proverbs and analogies to anyone who would listen.

Initially there appears to be no clear relationship with the respective career choices; however, while the fields were different, what each of us brought was not. My teaching style, explicit, direct, caring, truthful, and loving, was developed while listening to my grandmother day after day speaking to the Lincoln University students in the restaurant. I will always feel this is true. I did not realize until after my grandmother's transition how much we were alike. In fact, it was my assistant who pointed out the similarities.

My grandmother kept motivational sayings on three-by-five cards all around the restaurant and her home. When the cards became selectively invisible to a student, she recited them. I found a lot of three-by-five cards when I cleaned her house after she transitioned. I read through the cards, and I imagined where she placed the thought-provoking cards throughout the restaurant.

My grandmother spent time mentoring young men in the community. She provided the same message to them as she did the young Lincoln University students, get an education and do things right the first time. She hired the young men when no one else would; some of them were in and out of jail. In fact, a few of them stole from her. She showed them unconditional love when she would continue to pay them even after she knew they had broken in to her restaurant. She fed them food, nourishing their body and soul. Each would return to visit, once he had gotten his life together.

I currently live in my grandmother's house. She trusted me with her life's work and legacy. I am preserving the legacy and loving every minute.

A few days ago the house phone rang, and a man said, "Is Sissy there? May I speak to Sissy please?" I paused. Initially, I thought someone is playing a joke on me.

I replied in a harsh tone, "Stop playing! Who is this?" The gentleman said, "Excuse me, may I speak to Sissy please?" Lowering my voice and tension, I asked, "Who's calling?"

"Ja Jahannes. Is my friend home?"

"Ja, it is Lenetta."

"Hi, Lenetta, where is Sissy?"

"Ja, she is gone. She transitioned a little over a year ago." There was silence between us. "Oh my, my friend is gone," he finally replied. Ja told me he was thinking of her and wanted to see how she was doing. I reassured him she was doing well. We each agreed she was a beautiful woman.

Ja, a gifted storyteller and writer, recited several stories about my grandmother while we were on the phone. He told me how caring my grandmother was with the Lincoln University student body and how she did not take any mess. He informed me, like so many others, she fed him when he was broke and hungry. I remember so clearly my grandmother preaching life lessons to students who relied on her for nourishment. The story made me think of how I interact with my elementary school age students and my college students now.

Ja continued to tell me that he was working on a memoir of the Lincoln University poets, and he could not think of the name of the local bar. I spoke up and said, "The Rose Bowl." "Yes, that is right," he said. I could see Ja smiling through the phone. He continued, "So how are you?"

My grandmother introduced Ja and me several years ago when I was a tenured faculty member in the Education Department at Lincoln University. I told Ja I was writing a memoir about seven American women who stretched my heart. Interestingly enough, he said he recently presented on the same topic, and the response was overwhelming.

Nana Fanny's house will always be home to the immediate family and others. Throughout my life, I became impregnated by her caring attitude and her businesslike attitude toward life. All my life my grandmother socialized me to be me. Nana Fanny would say when you learn, you teach.

There is an old saying that suggests there are advantages to being both young and old: "The old palm fronds have defined and strengthen the tree, but the young palm fronds, building on the base, must find their meaning in pushing forward further and higher."

Nana Fanny defined and strengthened the tree; my job is to build on the foundation she established and find meaning in my identity and culture while moving higher and higher.

My grandmother is a mythoform for me to follow.

CONCLUSION

"If you are willing to be where you are."

With each mother, my heart grew, and so did my agency. I became the subject of my own story. While my other mothers were developing a relationship with me, I was developing a relationship with myself. My other mothers caused my heart to feel even all over. Their daily lessons led me to rational thought and action. My other mothers provided for me an expanded giving of self and sacrifice for me to experience freedom.

I am at home in my body, intuitive. As each mother planted seeds in me, I fell in love. I fell in love with the way the seeds germinated inside me, making me feel beautiful, inside and out, like the African sense of beauty. My seven other mothers possessed seven virtues: love, balance, patience, sacrifice, trust, sensitivity, and thoughtfulness. Each attribute poured in me; I drank and became impregnated with the seven virtues. I believed in the transformation. I model the seven virtues, and I pour the seven virtues in to my family.

Because of my other mothers, I remember who I am. I am present. I am awake; I am mindful. I am free.

My other mothers awakened a *sukha-manas* or joyous mind. It is my responsibility to maintain my joyous mind. With a joyful mind, interests in ego-enticing possessions diminish and confidence, optimism, and contentment flourish. To honor my other mothers, I honor myself.

If the community is living, breathing, we must all accept the responsibility of Divine Motherhood even for a moment. We must keep the younger generation close to us, and we must allow others to be their other mothers. This system can only happen if we are balanced.

It is my fervent hope that these words will trigger something inside. In most cases, we wait for a tragedy, a health issue, an accident, or death before we begin to think about living; consider living now.

My story of a road to freedom is so simple yet so profound. The value in my mothers' teachings is profound; I did not spend time unlearning pertinent life lessons. My other mothers' legacy is a lesson in moral instruction, a lesson that can be duplicated.

My seven other mothers created a joyful mind and a self-mastered person. Wisdom is the ultimate goal; wisdom is a concept that must flourish, for the younger generation, to evolve and achieve. Wisdom allows individuals and community to thrive. In some instances, it appears we are afraid to be wise. Wisdom speaks to reclaiming, embracing, and practicing rituals. Wisdom is essential to living a joyous life.

Along this path of knowledge, I began to understand my divine potential. Change for me became unconscious, a way of life, and there was a lack of fear.

Life is a sequence and a precious journey. The secret to life is to awaken before death and then realize there is no death. Truly, today is all there is. If not NOW, when?

EPILOGUE

Teach only love, for that is what you are.

By consistently transforming, we become wise. By consistently living in the moment, we free ourselves of past or future worries. By consistently being self-compassionate, we manage our daily lives. By consistently identifying, we develop a sound knowledge and appreciation of who we are and who we are becoming. By consistently practicing mindfulness, we make informed decisions. By consistently learning from past mistakes, we continue to grow, ridding ourselves of the contradictions that hold our souls and manage our actions. By consistently practicing daily mediation and rituals, we become socialized within our own circle of memory. By consistently being fully awake, we obtain insightfulness and intuition. By consistently being reflective, we refrain from material gain.

A joyous lifestyle is the life goal. A joyful state is the true nature. Each of us is the Egyptian lotus.

For information about lectures and workshops, contact
Lenetta Raysha Lee
1501 Baltimore Pike
Lincoln University, PA 19352
Telephone: 610-932-2734
    Email: Lenetta.Raysha.Lee@gmail.com

www.ingramcontent.com/pod-product-compliance
Lightning Source LLC
Chambersburg PA
CBHW050340290526
45785CB00006B/2578